Nurturing Naturally, Home Remedies for Kids

Diverne Ingraham

publisher logo

NURTURING NATURALLY, HOME REMEDIES FOR KIDS

Nurturing Naturally: A Parent's Guide to Home Remedies for Kids

ISBN: 979-8-8689-5798-7

Published by DLK Publishing
1655 Prudential Dr
Jacksonville FL 32207
U.S.A

Cover design by Kristian Ingraham

Editor: LaCher Abril Ingraham

Printed in U.S.A

Second Edition, 2024

For more information about the author, visit **Amazon.com/author/diverneji**

HEALTH DISCLAIMER

Health Disclaimer

The information provided in this book is intended for educational and informational purposes only. It is not a substitute for professional medical advice, diagnosis, or treatment. Always seek the advice of your physician, pediatrician, or other qualified healthcare provider with any questions you may have regarding a medical condition or health concern.

Important Points to Consider:

1. **Consult Healthcare Providers**: Before starting any new treatment or remedy, including those mentioned in this book, it is essential to consult with a healthcare professional, especially for children, pregnant women, individuals with existing health conditions, or those taking medications.

2. **Individual Differences**: Every individual is unique, and what works for one person may not work for another. Factors such as age, health status, allergies, and individual sensitivities can affect the suitability and effectiveness of any remedy.

3. **Safety First**: Use caution when applying natural remedies, especially when using essential oils, herbs, or supplements. Ensure proper dilution, dosage, and administration to avoid adverse reactions. Always perform a patch test before using any new topical product on your child's skin.

4. **Emergency Situations**: In case of a medical emergency or if you have concerns about your child's health, seek immediate medical attention. This book is not intended to provide emergency medical care or to replace professional medical advice.

5. **Accuracy of Information**: While every effort has been made to ensure the accuracy and completeness of the information in this book, medical knowledge and understanding of health

practices are constantly evolving. The author and publisher are not responsible for any errors, omissions, or outcomes related to the use of this information.

6. **Personal Responsibility**: The reader assumes full responsibility for using the information in this book. The author and publisher disclaim any liability arising directly or indirectly from the use or application of any of the contents of this book.

This disclaimer is intended to ensure that readers use the information provided responsibly and in conjunction with professional medical advice. Always prioritize the health and safety of your family by making informed decisions and consulting with healthcare professionals as needed.

TABLE OF CONTENT

INTRODUCTION

The Importance of Natural Remedies

The use of natural remedies for children is an age-old practice that has been handed down through generations. These remedies are not only rooted in tradition but also in the wisdom of natural healing. They offer an alternative or complement to conventional medicine, providing a gentle and holistic approach to health and wellness. For many parents, the appeal of natural remedies lies in their ability to treat common ailments without the side effects often associated with pharmaceutical drugs.

One of the primary benefits of natural remedies is their holistic nature. Rather than targeting a specific symptom, many natural treatments address the root cause of an ailment and promote overall well-being. For instance, a cup of chamomile tea might not only soothe a child's upset stomach but also help them relax and sleep better. This holistic approach can be particularly beneficial for children, whose developing bodies and minds are sensitive to strong medications.

Natural remedies also empower parents to take an active role in their children's health. By learning about and applying these remedies, parents can become more attuned to their children's needs and better equipped to address minor health issues at home. This can lead to a greater sense of confidence and control over their family's health and well-being.

Moreover, the use of natural remedies encourages a closer connection to nature. Many of these remedies involve the use of herbs, plants, and other natural ingredients, fostering an appreciation for the natural world. This can be an invaluable lesson for children, teaching them about the importance of sustainability and the benefits of living in harmony with nature.

The History and Tradition of Home Remedies

Home remedies have a rich history that spans across cultures and continents. From the ancient Egyptians to the traditional Chinese, various civilizations have developed their own systems of natural medicine. These practices were often based on a deep understanding of the natural world and a keen observation of how different plants and substances affected the human body.

In many cultures, the knowledge of home remedies was passed down orally from one generation to the next. Grandmothers and mothers often served as the primary custodians of this knowledge, using their wisdom to care for their families and communities. This tradition continues in many parts of the world today, where natural remedies are still the first line of defense against common ailments.

One of the most well-documented systems of natural medicine is Traditional Chinese Medicine (TCM), which has been practiced for thousands of years. TCM includes the use of herbal medicine, acupuncture, and dietary therapy, among other modalities. Similarly, Ayurveda, the traditional medicine system of India, offers a comprehensive approach to health that includes herbal treatments, dietary recommendations, and lifestyle practices.

In the Western world, the use of natural remedies can be traced back to ancient Greece and Rome. Hippocrates, often referred to as the "father of medicine," emphasized the healing power of nature and the importance of a balanced diet, exercise, and rest. This philosophy laid the foundation for much of modern natural medicine.

The Benefits Over Conventional Medicine

While conventional medicine has made tremendous advancements and offers life-saving treatments, it is not without its limitations. Many parents are concerned about the potential side effects of pharmaceutical drugs, particularly when used frequently or over long periods. Natural remedies, on the other hand, are generally considered to be gentler and have fewer side effects.

For example, many parents turn to natural remedies to avoid the overuse of antibiotics, which can lead to antibiotic resistance and disrupt the natural balance of bacteria in the gut. Natural remedies can offer effective alternatives for treating minor infections and boosting the immune system without these risks.

Another significant benefit of natural remedies is their cost-effectiveness. Many natural treatments can be made at home using simple, inexpensive ingredients. This can be particularly important for families with limited access to healthcare or those looking to reduce their medical expenses.

Natural remedies also encourage a more proactive approach to health. By focusing on prevention and the maintenance of overall well-being, these remedies can help reduce the incidence of illness in the first place. This contrasts with the more reactive approach of conventional medicine, which often focuses on treating symptoms after they have already developed.

Safety Considerations

While natural remedies offer many benefits, it is essential to use them safely and responsibly, especially when it comes to children. Not all natural remedies are appropriate for every child, and some can cause allergic reactions or interact with other medications. It is always best to consult with a healthcare professional before trying a new remedy, particularly for serious or persistent conditions.

Parents should also be aware of the proper dosages and preparation methods for natural remedies. Children's bodies are smaller and more sensitive than adults', so they require different dosages and formulations. It is crucial to follow recipes and guidelines carefully to ensure the safety and effectiveness of the remedies.

Moreover, parents should always be vigilant for signs of adverse reactions. Even natural substances can cause side effects or allergic reactions in some individuals. If a child experiences any unusual symptoms after taking a natural remedy, it is important to discontinue use and seek medical advice.

Finally, natural remedies should be seen as a complement to, rather than a replacement for, conventional medical care. While they can be highly effective for minor ailments and preventive care, serious or life-threatening conditions require professional medical treatment. By integrating natural remedies with conventional medicine, parents can provide the best possible care for their children.

The Structure of This Book

This book is designed to be a comprehensive guide to using natural remedies for children's health. Each chapter focuses on a specific area of health, providing detailed information on common ailments and the natural remedies that can help. The chapters are organized to make it easy for parents to find the information they need quickly and efficiently.

In Chapter 1, we will explore natural remedies for common ailments such as fever, colds, and stomach aches. These are some of the most frequent health issues that children face, and natural remedies can offer effective relief without the need for pharmaceuticals.

Chapter 2 delves into skin conditions, including diaper rash, eczema, and minor cuts and scrapes. The skin is the body's largest organ, and keeping it healthy is crucial for overall well-being.

Respiratory issues, such as nasal congestion, allergies, and asthma, are covered in Chapter 3. These conditions can be particularly challenging for children, but natural remedies can provide significant relief and support respiratory health.

Digestive problems, including constipation, indigestion, and colic, are addressed in Chapter 4. A healthy digestive system is essential for overall health, and natural remedies can help maintain digestive balance.

In Chapter 5, we will look at sleep issues, including insomnia, nightmares, and restlessness. Good sleep is vital for a child's development and well-being, and natural remedies can promote better sleep patterns.

Boosting immunity is the focus of Chapter 6. A strong immune system is the best defense against illness, and natural remedies can support and enhance immune function.

Chapter 7 explores behavioral and emotional health, including anxiety, hyperactivity, and mood swings. Natural remedies can play a significant role in supporting mental and emotional well-being in children.

Preventive care is covered in Chapter 8. This chapter emphasizes the importance of regular check-ups, vaccinations, and good hygiene practices, and how these can be complemented with natural remedies.

First aid and safety are the focus of Chapter 9. Knowing how to handle minor injuries and emergencies with natural remedies can be incredibly empowering for parents.

Finally, Chapter 10 provides recipes and DIY remedies, including herbal teas, homemade balms, and natural cleaning products. These practical guides make it easy for parents to create their own natural remedies at home.

Encouraging Parental Involvement

One of the key themes of this book is the importance of parental involvement in children's health. By learning about natural remedies and how to use them, parents can take a more active role in their children's care. This not only helps ensure the best possible outcomes for their health but also strengthens the bond between parent and child.

Teaching children about natural remedies can also empower them to take charge of their own health as they grow older. By involving them in the preparation and use of these remedies, parents can instill valuable lessons about self-care and the benefits of natural health practices.

Natural remedies offer a safe, effective, and holistic approach to children's health. By understanding and using these remedies, parents can provide gentle and nurturing care for their children, promoting overall well-being and preventing illness. This book aims to be a comprehensive guide, offering practical information and advice to help parents integrate natural remedies into their family's healthcare routine.

The journey to natural healing is a rewarding one, filled with the wisdom of tradition and the promise of better health. By embracing this approach, parents can foster a healthier, happier future for their children.

1

COMMON AILMENTS AND NATURAL REMEDIES

Fever

Fever is a common response of the body to infections. It is a natural defense mechanism that helps the immune system fight off pathogens. However, it can be distressing for both children and parents. While over-the-counter medications like acetaminophen or ibuprofen are commonly used, there are several natural remedies that can help reduce fever and provide comfort to a sick child.

Herbal Teas One effective remedy for fever is herbal tea. Chamomile, peppermint, and elderflower teas are particularly beneficial. These herbs have anti-inflammatory and soothing properties that can help lower body temperature. To prepare, steep one teaspoon of dried herb (or one tea bag) in a cup of hot water for 5-10 minutes. Allow it to cool to a comfortable temperature before giving it to the child.

Cool Compresses Applying a cool, damp washcloth to the forehead, wrists, and ankles can help reduce fever. This method works by drawing heat away from the body. It's important to use lukewarm water rather than cold, as using cold water can cause the body to shiver and potentially raise the temperature further.

Hydration Keeping a child hydrated is crucial when they have a fever. Fever can lead to dehydration, so offering plenty of fluids is essential. Water, clear broths, herbal teas, and electrolyte solutions are good options. Avoid sugary drinks and caffeinated beverages, which can contribute to dehydration.

Rest Rest is vital for recovery. Encourage your child to rest as much as possible. Create a comfortable resting environment with soft blankets and pillows. Reading stories or playing quiet games can help keep them calm and entertained while they recover.

Apple Cider Vinegar Apple cider vinegar is another traditional remedy for fever. It is believed to help draw out heat from the body. Mix one part apple cider vinegar with two parts water, soak a washcloth in the mixture, and place it on the child's forehead or abdomen. The vinegar's cooling effect can help reduce fever.

Ginger Bath A ginger bath can help reduce fever by promoting sweating, which helps cool the body down. Add a few slices of fresh ginger to a warm bath and let your child soak for 10-15 minutes. Ensure the bathwater is warm, not hot, to avoid increasing the body temperature.

Monitoring and Seeking Help While natural remedies can be effective, it's important to monitor the fever closely. If the fever is very high (above 104°F or 40°C), persistent, or accompanied by other severe symptoms such as difficulty breathing, persistent vomiting, or a rash, seek medical attention immediately. Fever in infants under three months should always be evaluated by a healthcare provider.

Colds and Flu

Colds and flu are common viral infections that can cause a range of symptoms, including congestion, runny nose, cough, sore throat, and fatigue. While there is no cure for these illnesses, natural remedies can help alleviate symptoms and support the body's immune system.

Honey and Lemon Honey is a natural cough suppressant and can soothe a sore throat. Lemon is rich in vitamin C, which can help boost the immune system. To make a soothing drink, mix one tablespoon of honey and the juice of half a lemon in a cup of warm water. Give this to your child several times a day. Note: Honey should not be given to children under one year old due to the risk of botulism.

Steam Inhalation Steam inhalation can help relieve nasal congestion and soothe irritated airways. Boil a pot of water, remove it from the heat, and let it cool slightly. Have your child sit with their face over the pot, covering their head with a towel to trap the steam. Instruct them to breathe deeply for 5-10 minutes. Adding a few drops of eucalyptus or peppermint oil can enhance the benefits.

Elderberry Syrup Elderberry has antiviral properties and can help reduce the duration and severity of colds and flu. Elderberry syrup can be purchased or made at home by simmering elderberries with water, straining the mixture, and adding honey. Give your child a teaspoon of elderberry syrup several times a day.

Chicken Soup Chicken soup is a classic remedy for colds and flu. It provides hydration, essential nutrients, and has mild anti-inflammatory properties. The steam from the hot soup can also help clear nasal passages. Make a nutritious chicken soup with plenty of vegetables and herbs like garlic and thyme for added immune support.

Garlic Garlic has antiviral and immune-boosting properties. Adding garlic to your child's diet can help fight off colds and flu. You can incorporate garlic into soups, broths, or even make a garlic-infused honey by crushing a few cloves of garlic and mixing them with honey. Let it sit for a few hours and give a small spoonful to your child.

Hydration and Rest Ensuring your child stays hydrated is crucial. Offer plenty of fluids such as water, herbal teas, and clear broths. Rest is also essential for recovery, so encourage your child to take it easy and get plenty of sleep.

Saline Nasal Spray A saline nasal spray can help relieve nasal congestion by moisturizing and clearing the nasal passages. You can make a simple saline solution at home by dissolving a teaspoon of salt in a cup of warm water. Use a dropper or nasal spray bottle to administer a few drops into each nostril.

Cough

Coughing is a common symptom of respiratory infections and can be particularly bothersome for children, disrupting sleep and causing discomfort. Natural remedies can help soothe the throat, reduce irritation, and support the body's healing process.

Ginger Syrup Ginger has anti-inflammatory and antimicrobial properties that can help alleviate coughing. To make ginger syrup, simmer sliced fresh ginger in water until the liquid reduces by half. Strain the ginger and mix the liquid with honey. Give your child a teaspoon of this syrup several times a day to soothe their cough.

Onion and Honey Mixture Onions have expectorant properties that can help loosen mucus and ease coughing. Chop an onion and mix it with honey. Let it sit for a few hours until the onion releases its juice. Give your child a teaspoon of the mixture several times a day. This remedy can be surprisingly effective in reducing cough.

Thyme Tea Thyme is known for its antitussive (cough suppressing) properties. To make thyme tea, steep one teaspoon of dried thyme in a cup of hot water for 10 minutes. Strain and let it cool before giving it to your child. This tea can help soothe the throat and reduce coughing.

Marshmallow Root Tea Marshmallow root contains mucilage, which can coat and soothe the throat. To prepare marshmallow root tea, steep one tablespoon of dried marshmallow root in a cup of hot water for 15-20 minutes. Strain and allow it to cool before giving it to your child. This tea can provide relief from a persistent cough.

Licorice Root Licorice root has soothing and anti-inflammatory properties. You can make a tea by steeping one teaspoon of dried licorice root in a cup of hot water for 10 minutes. Strain and let it cool before giving it to your child. Licorice root tea can help reduce coughing and soothe an irritated throat.

Honey and Warm Water A simple mixture of honey and warm water can help soothe a sore throat and reduce coughing. Mix one tablespoon of honey in a cup of warm water and give it to your child several times a day. The honey coats the throat and provides relief from irritation.

Humidifier Using a humidifier in your child's room can help keep the air moist, reducing throat irritation and coughing. This is particularly helpful at night when dry air can worsen a cough. Make sure to clean the humidifier regularly to prevent the growth of mold and bacteria.

Sore Throat

A sore throat can be caused by viral or bacterial infections, allergies, or environmental irritants. It can make swallowing painful and uncomfortable. Natural remedies can provide relief by soothing the throat and reducing inflammation.

Saltwater Gargle A saltwater gargle is a simple and effective remedy for a sore throat. Mix half a teaspoon of salt in a glass of warm water and have your child gargle with it several times a day. The salt helps reduce inflammation and kill bacteria, providing relief from pain and irritation.

Chamomile Tea Chamomile has anti-inflammatory and soothing properties that can help ease a sore throat. Steep one teaspoon of dried chamomile flowers in a cup of hot water for 5-10 minutes. Strain and let it cool before giving it to your child. Adding a bit of honey can enhance its soothing effect.

Marshmallow Root Tea Marshmallow root can coat the throat and provide relief from soreness. Steep one tablespoon of dried marshmallow root in a cup of hot water for 15-20 minutes. Strain and allow it to cool before giving it to your child. This tea can help reduce throat irritation and pain.

Slippery Elm Lozenges Slippery elm contains mucilage, which can coat and soothe the throat. Slippery elm lozenges are available in health food stores and can be given to children to suck on throughout the day. These lozenges can provide relief from a sore throat and help with swallowing.

Honey and Warm Water Honey is a natural antibacterial and can help soothe a sore throat. Mix one tablespoon of honey in a cup of warm water and give it to your child several times a day. The honey coats the throat and provides relief from irritation. Remember not to give honey to children under one year old.

Hydration Keeping your child hydrated is important when they have a sore throat. Offer plenty of fluids such as water, herbal teas, and clear broths. Warm liquids can be particularly soothing for a sore throat.

Rest Encourage your child to rest and avoid talking or shouting, which can further irritate the throat. Creating a calm and quiet environment can help speed up recovery.

Stomach Ache

Stomach aches can be caused by a variety of factors, including indigestion, gas, constipation, or stomach infections. Natural remedies can help alleviate the discomfort and address the underlying causes.

Peppermint Tea Peppermint has antispasmodic properties that can help relax the muscles of the digestive tract and relieve stomach pain. Steep one teaspoon of dried peppermint leaves in a cup of hot water for 5-10 minutes. Strain and let it cool before giving it to your child. This tea can help alleviate indigestion and gas.

Warm Compress A warm compress can provide relief from stomach aches by relaxing the abdominal muscles and reducing cramps. Use a warm water bottle or a warm towel and place it on your child's stomach for 10-15 minutes. Ensure the compress is warm, not hot, to avoid burns.

Ginger Tea Ginger is known for its digestive benefits and can help reduce nausea and stomach pain. To make ginger tea, slice a small piece of fresh ginger and simmer it in a cup of water for 10-15 minutes. Strain and let it cool before giving it to your child. This tea can help soothe the stomach and relieve pain.

Fennel Seeds Fennel seeds have carminative properties that can help reduce gas and bloating. Crush a teaspoon of fennel seeds and steep them in a cup of hot water for 10 minutes. Strain and let it cool before giving it to your child. Fennel tea can help alleviate stomach aches and improve digestion.

Bananas Bananas are easy to digest and can help soothe an upset stomach. They are also rich in potassium, which can help restore electrolyte balance if your child has been vomiting or has diarrhea. Offer ripe bananas to your child as a gentle food option.

Yogurt Yogurt contains probiotics, which can help restore the balance of good bacteria in the gut. This can be particularly helpful if your child's stomach ache is caused by an infection or after taking antibiotics. Choose plain, unsweetened yogurt and offer it to your child as a snack.

Hydration Ensuring your child stays hydrated is important, especially if they have been vomiting or have diarrhea. Offer small sips of water, clear broths, or oral rehydration solutions to maintain hydration and electrolyte balance.

Diarrhea

Diarrhea is characterized by frequent, loose, or watery stools. It can be caused by infections, food intolerances, or digestive disorders. Natural remedies can help manage symptoms and prevent dehydration.

BRAT Diet The BRAT diet (Bananas, Rice, Applesauce, Toast) is a traditional remedy for diarrhea. These foods are bland, easy to digest, and can help firm up stools. Offer small, frequent meals of these foods to your child until their diarrhea improves.

Oral Rehydration Solution Dehydration is a major concern with diarrhea, so keeping your child hydrated is crucial. An oral rehydration solution can help replace lost fluids and electrolytes. You can make a simple solution at home by mixing 1 liter of water with 6 teaspoons of sugar and 1/2 teaspoon of salt. Offer small sips frequently.

Probiotics Probiotics can help restore the balance of good bacteria in the gut and improve digestive health. Yogurt, kefir, and probiotic supplements can be beneficial for children with diarrhea. Choose products with live and active cultures for the best results.

Chamomile Tea Chamomile has anti-inflammatory and soothing properties that can help reduce intestinal spasms and diarrhea. Steep one teaspoon of dried chamomile flowers in a cup of hot water for 5-10 minutes. Strain and let it cool before giving it to your child. Chamomile tea can help calm the digestive system.

Apple Cider Vinegar Apple cider vinegar can help restore the natural pH balance of the digestive tract and improve symptoms of diarrhea. Mix one teaspoon of apple cider vinegar in a glass of water and give it to your child several times a day. This remedy can help firm up stools and improve digestion.

Blueberry Soup Blueberries contain anthocyanins, which have antimicrobial properties and can help reduce diarrhea. You can make a simple blueberry soup by simmering fresh or frozen blueberries with water until they soften. Blend the mixture and let it cool before offering it to your child.

Rest and Monitoring Encourage your child to rest and avoid strenuous activities while they recover. Monitor their symptoms closely, and seek medical attention if they show signs of severe dehydration, such as dry mouth, sunken eyes, or decreased urine output, or if the diarrhea persists for more than a few days.

2

SKIN CONDITIONS

Diaper Rash

Diaper rash is a common skin condition in infants and toddlers, characterized by red, inflamed skin in the diaper area. It can be caused by prolonged exposure to wet or dirty diapers, chafing, or sensitivity to diaper materials. Natural remedies can help soothe and heal the skin effectively.

Coconut Oil Coconut oil has antibacterial and antifungal properties, making it an excellent remedy for diaper rash. It also provides a protective barrier that keeps the skin moisturized. After cleaning and drying your baby's diaper area, apply a thin layer of coconut oil to the affected area. This can help reduce inflammation and promote healing.

Oatmeal Baths Oatmeal has soothing and anti-inflammatory properties that can help relieve diaper rash. To prepare an oatmeal bath, grind a cup of plain, uncooked oats into a fine powder using a blender or food processor. Add the oatmeal powder to a warm bath and let your baby soak for 10-15 minutes. Pat the skin dry gently after the bath.

Aloe Vera Aloe vera is known for its soothing and healing properties. Apply a small amount of pure aloe vera gel to the affected area to help reduce redness and irritation. Ensure that the gel is 100% pure without added chemicals or fragrances.

Breast Milk Breast milk contains antibodies and other healing properties that can help treat diaper rash. Applying a few drops of breast milk to the affected area and allowing it to air dry can provide relief and promote healing. This is a gentle and natural option, especially for breastfeeding mothers.

Calendula Cream Calendula is a medicinal herb known for its anti-inflammatory and healing properties. Calendula cream can be applied to the diaper area to soothe and heal the skin. Ensure that the cream is free from harsh chemicals and fragrances.

Air Time Allowing your baby some diaper-free time can help the skin breathe and heal faster. Let your baby play without a diaper for a few minutes several times a day. Place a soft, absorbent towel or blanket underneath to catch any accidents.

Proper Diapering Practices Changing diapers frequently is essential to prevent and treat diaper rash. Ensure the diaper area is clean and dry before putting on a new diaper. Use gentle, fragrance-free wipes or a soft cloth with warm water to clean the area. Avoid using wipes with alcohol or harsh chemicals that can irritate the skin.

Eczema

Eczema, or atopic dermatitis, is a chronic skin condition characterized by dry, itchy, and inflamed skin. It often appears in children and can be triggered by allergens, irritants, or genetic factors. Natural remedies can help manage and soothe eczema symptoms.

Aloe Vera Aloe vera gel can provide relief from the itching and inflammation associated with eczema. Apply a thin layer of pure aloe vera gel to the affected areas to soothe the skin. Ensure that the gel is free from additives and fragrances.

Coconut Oil Coconut oil is an excellent moisturizer and can help soothe dry, itchy skin. Apply a thin layer of coconut oil to the affected areas after bathing, when the skin is still damp, to lock in moisture. The antibacterial properties of coconut oil can also help prevent infections in the irritated skin.

Oatmeal Baths An oatmeal bath can provide relief from itching and inflammation. Grind a cup of plain, uncooked oats into a fine powder and add it to a warm bath. Let your child soak for 10-15 minutes. After the bath, pat the skin dry gently and apply a moisturizer.

Chamomile Tea Compress Chamomile has anti-inflammatory and soothing properties that can help reduce eczema symptoms. Brew a cup of chamomile tea, let it cool, and use a soft cloth to apply the tea to the affected areas. This can help soothe itching and inflammation.

Shea Butter Shea butter is a natural moisturizer that can help soothe and heal eczema-affected skin. Apply a small amount of pure shea butter to the affected areas to keep the skin hydrated and reduce inflammation. Look for unrefined, raw shea butter for the best results.

Honey Honey has natural antibacterial and anti-inflammatory properties. Applying a thin layer of raw honey to the affected areas can help soothe and heal eczema patches. Leave it on for 20-30 minutes before gently rinsing it off with warm water.

Dietary Considerations Sometimes, eczema can be triggered or worsened by certain foods. Keeping a food diary and noting any flare-ups can help identify potential triggers. Common allergens include dairy, eggs, nuts, and gluten. Consulting with a healthcare professional or a nutritionist can help determine if dietary changes are needed.

Hydration Keeping the skin hydrated is essential in managing eczema. Encourage your child to drink plenty of water throughout the day. Applying moisturizers regularly, especially after bathing, can help maintain skin hydration.

Minor Cuts and Scrapes

Children are prone to minor cuts and scrapes as they explore and play. Proper care and natural remedies can help prevent infection and promote healing.

Cleaning the Wound The first step in treating a cut or scrape is to clean the wound thoroughly. Rinse the area with clean, running water to remove dirt and debris. Use a mild soap if needed, and pat the area dry with a clean towel. Avoid using harsh antiseptics that can irritate the skin.

Honey Honey has natural antibacterial properties and can promote healing. Apply a thin layer of raw honey to the clean wound and cover it with a sterile bandage. Change the bandage and reapply honey daily until the wound heals.

Turmeric Paste Turmeric is known for its anti-inflammatory and antibacterial properties. Make a paste by mixing turmeric powder with a small amount of water or coconut oil. Apply the paste to the clean wound and cover it with a bandage. Turmeric can help reduce inflammation and prevent infection.

Aloe Vera Aloe vera gel can soothe and heal minor cuts and scrapes. Apply a thin layer of pure aloe vera gel to the clean wound. Aloe vera can help reduce inflammation, prevent infection, and promote healing.

Calendula Ointment Calendula is a medicinal herb with healing properties. Calendula ointment can be applied to minor cuts and scrapes to promote healing and reduce inflammation. Ensure the ointment is free from harsh chemicals and fragrances.

Lavender Essential Oil Lavender essential oil has antiseptic and healing properties. Dilute a few drops of lavender essential oil with a carrier oil, such as coconut or olive oil, and apply it to the clean wound. Lavender oil can help prevent infection and promote healing.

Coconut Oil Coconut oil has moisturizing and antibacterial properties. Applying a thin layer of coconut oil to the clean wound can help keep the area moist and prevent infection. Coconut oil can also promote healing and reduce scarring.

Proper Wound Care Keep the wound clean and covered with a sterile bandage to prevent infection. Change the bandage daily or whenever it becomes dirty or wet. Monitor the wound for signs of infection, such as increased redness, swelling, or pus. If you notice any signs of infection, seek medical attention promptly.

Insect Bites and Stings

Insect bites and stings are common in children and can cause itching, swelling, and discomfort. Natural remedies can help soothe the skin and reduce inflammation.

Baking Soda Paste Baking soda can help neutralize the venom from insect bites and stings and reduce itching and swelling. Make a paste by mixing baking soda with a small amount of water. Apply the paste to the affected area and let it sit for 10-15 minutes before rinsing it off with cool water.

Aloe Vera Aloe vera gel can provide relief from itching and inflammation caused by insect bites and stings. Apply a thin layer of pure aloe vera gel to the affected area. Aloe vera can soothe the skin and promote healing.

Lavender Essential Oil Lavender essential oil has anti-inflammatory and soothing properties. Dilute a few drops of lavender essential oil with a carrier oil, such as coconut or olive oil, and apply it to the affected area. Lavender oil can help reduce itching and swelling.

Tea Tree Oil Tea tree oil has antiseptic and anti-inflammatory properties. Dilute a few drops of tea tree oil with a carrier oil and apply it to the affected area. Tea tree oil can help prevent infection and reduce inflammation.

Apple Cider Vinegar Apple cider vinegar can help relieve itching and reduce inflammation. Dilute apple cider vinegar with an equal amount of water and apply it to the affected area using a cotton ball. This remedy can help neutralize the venom and soothe the skin.

Honey Honey has natural antibacterial and anti-inflammatory properties. Apply a thin layer of raw honey to the affected area to reduce itching and swelling. Honey can also help prevent infection and promote healing.

Basil Leaves Basil leaves contain compounds that can help relieve itching. Crush fresh basil leaves and apply the paste to the affected area. Leave it on for a few minutes before rinsing it off with cool water. This remedy can provide relief from itching and inflammation.

Ice Pack Applying an ice pack to the affected area can help reduce swelling and numb the skin, providing relief from itching and pain. Wrap ice in a cloth or use a cold pack and apply it to the bite or sting for 10-15 minutes. Do not apply ice directly to the skin to avoid frostbite.

Burns

Minor burns can occur from hot surfaces, liquids, or sun exposure. Proper care and natural remedies can help soothe the skin and promote healing.

Aloe Vera Aloe vera is one of the most effective natural remedies for burns. Its gel has soothing and healing properties that can help reduce pain and inflammation. Apply pure aloe vera gel directly to the burn and let it dry. Repeat several times a day to promote healing.

Honey Honey has natural antibacterial and anti-inflammatory properties. Applying a thin layer of raw honey to a minor burn can help prevent infection and soothe the skin. Cover the burn with a sterile bandage and change it daily.

Cool Water Running cool (not cold) water over a burn for 10-15 minutes can help reduce pain and swelling. Avoid using ice, as it can cause further damage to the skin. After cooling the burn, pat the area dry gently.

Lavender Essential Oil Lavender essential oil has antiseptic and healing properties. Dilute a few drops of lavender essential oil with a carrier oil, such as coconut or olive oil, and apply it to the burn. Lavender oil can help reduce pain and promote healing.

Coconut Oil Coconut oil has moisturizing and antibacterial properties that can help soothe and heal minor burns. After cooling the burn, apply a thin layer of coconut oil to the affected area. Coconut oil can help keep the skin moisturized and prevent infection.

Calendula Ointment Calendula is a medicinal herb with healing properties. Applying calendula ointment to a minor burn can help reduce inflammation and promote healing. Ensure the ointment is free from harsh chemicals and fragrances.

Potato Slices Potato slices can help soothe minor burns and reduce pain. Slice a raw potato and place the slices directly on the burn. Leave them on for a few minutes before removing. The cooling effect of the potato can provide relief from the burn.

Oatmeal Baths An oatmeal bath can help soothe sunburned skin. Grind a cup of plain, uncooked oats into a fine powder and add it to a cool bath. Let your child soak for 10-15 minutes. After the bath, pat the skin dry gently and apply a moisturizer.

Prevention and Monitoring To prevent burns, keep hot liquids, appliances, and chemicals out of children's reach. Use sunscreen to protect your child from sunburn, and reapply it regularly when outdoors. Monitor burns for signs of infection, such as increased redness, swelling, or pus. If you notice any signs of infection or if the burn is severe, seek medical attention promptly.

3

RESPIRATORY ISSUES

Nasal Congestion

Nasal congestion is a common issue in children, especially during cold and allergy seasons. It can cause discomfort, difficulty breathing, and disrupt sleep. Natural remedies can help relieve congestion and make it easier for your child to breathe.

Saline Drops Saline drops are a simple and effective remedy for nasal congestion. They work by thinning the mucus, making it easier to clear out. You can buy saline drops at a pharmacy or make them at home by dissolving a teaspoon of salt in a cup of warm water. Use a dropper to put a few drops of the solution into each nostril, then have your child gently blow their nose. This can be done several times a day to keep the nasal passages clear.

Eucalyptus Steam Eucalyptus steam inhalation can help clear nasal congestion by loosening mucus and opening the airways. To prepare eucalyptus steam, boil a pot of water and remove it from the heat. Add a few drops of eucalyptus essential oil to the water. Have your child sit with their face over the pot, covering their head with a towel to trap the steam. Instruct them to breathe deeply for 5-10 minutes. This remedy can be particularly effective before bedtime to help your child sleep better.

Hydration Keeping your child hydrated is essential for thinning mucus and relieving congestion. Encourage them to drink plenty of fluids, such as water, herbal teas, and clear broths. Warm liquids, in particular, can help soothe the throat and clear the nasal passages.

Warm Compress A warm compress applied to the face can help relieve nasal congestion by reducing inflammation and promoting drainage. Soak a clean cloth in warm water, wring out the excess, and place it over your child's nose and forehead. Leave it on for a few minutes, repeating as necessary.

Elevating the Head Elevating your child's head while they sleep can help reduce nasal congestion. Place a pillow or two under the mattress or use a wedge pillow to raise the head of the bed. This can help promote better drainage and make breathing easier.

Essential Oils Essential oils like peppermint and lavender can also help relieve nasal congestion. You can diffuse these oils in your child's room or add a few drops to a warm bath. The soothing vapors can help open up the airways and promote relaxation.

Allergies

Allergies can cause a range of respiratory issues, including nasal congestion, sneezing, and itchy eyes. Natural remedies can help manage allergy symptoms and reduce the body's sensitivity to allergens.

Quercetin-Rich Foods Quercetin is a natural antihistamine and anti-inflammatory compound found in many fruits and vegetables. Including quercetin-rich foods in your child's diet can help reduce allergy symptoms. Foods high in quercetin include apples, berries, grapes, onions, and broccoli. These foods can help stabilize mast cells and reduce the release of histamine, which is responsible for allergy symptoms.

Local Honey Local honey is believed to help reduce allergy symptoms by exposing the body to small amounts of local pollen, potentially building up immunity. Giving your child a teaspoon of local honey daily can help manage allergies. It's important to note that honey should not be given to children under one year old due to the risk of botulism.

Nettle Leaf Tea Nettle leaf has natural antihistamine properties and can help reduce inflammation and allergy symptoms. To make nettle leaf tea, steep one teaspoon of dried nettle leaf in a cup of hot water for 5-10 minutes. Strain and let it cool before giving it to your child. This tea can be taken daily during allergy season.

Butterbur Butterbur is an herb that can help reduce allergy symptoms. It acts as a natural antihistamine and can relieve nasal congestion and itching. Butterbur supplements are available in health food stores. It's important to choose a product that is free from pyrrolizidine alkaloids (PAs), which can be harmful to the liver.

Vitamin C Vitamin C is a natural antihistamine and immune booster. Including vitamin C-rich foods in your child's diet can help manage allergies. Foods high in vitamin C include citrus fruits, strawberries, kiwi, bell peppers, and leafy greens. Vitamin C supplements are also available, but it's best to consult with a healthcare professional before starting any new supplement.

Air Purifiers Using an air purifier in your child's room can help reduce airborne allergens, such as pollen, dust mites, and pet dander. Choose a purifier with a HEPA filter for the best results. Keeping windows closed during high pollen seasons and regularly cleaning your home can also help reduce allergen exposure.

Asthma

Asthma is a chronic respiratory condition characterized by inflammation and narrowing of the airways, leading to difficulty breathing, coughing, and wheezing. Natural remedies can help manage asthma symptoms and improve overall respiratory health.

Herbal Teas (Thyme, Licorice Root) Herbal teas can help soothe the airways and reduce inflammation. Thyme has antispasmodic properties that can help relax the bronchial muscles, while licorice root has anti-inflammatory and soothing effects.

Thyme Tea: Steep one teaspoon of dried thyme in a cup of hot water for 10 minutes. Strain and let it cool before giving it to your child. This tea can help reduce coughing and ease breathing.

Licorice Root Tea: Steep one teaspoon of dried licorice root in a cup of hot water for 10 minutes. Strain and let it cool before giving it to your child. Licorice root tea can help soothe the airways and reduce inflammation. Note: Licorice root should not be used for prolonged periods and is not recommended for children with high blood pressure.

Breathing Exercises Breathing exercises can help improve lung function and reduce asthma symptoms. Teaching your child simple breathing techniques can help them manage asthma attacks and improve their overall respiratory health.

Diaphragmatic Breathing: This exercise involves breathing deeply into the diaphragm rather than shallowly into the chest. Have your child lie on their back with one hand on their chest and the other on their abdomen. Instruct them to breathe in deeply through their nose, feeling their abdomen rise, and then exhale slowly through their mouth. Practicing this exercise regularly can help improve lung function.

Pursed-Lip Breathing: This technique helps keep the airways open longer, making it easier to breathe. Instruct your child to inhale deeply through their nose and then exhale slowly through pursed lips (as if they are blowing out a candle). This can be especially helpful during an asthma attack.

Essential Oils Essential oils like eucalyptus, peppermint, and lavender can help manage asthma symptoms. Eucalyptus oil, in particular, has decongestant properties that can help open up the airways. You can use a diffuser to disperse the oils in your child's room or add a few drops to a warm bath. Always dilute essential oils with a carrier oil before applying them to the skin, and consult with a healthcare professional before using essential oils for asthma.

Ginger Ginger has anti-inflammatory properties that can help reduce airway inflammation and improve asthma symptoms. Adding fresh ginger to your child's diet or giving them ginger tea can provide relief. To make ginger tea, slice a small piece of fresh ginger and simmer it in a cup of water for 10-15 minutes. Strain and let it cool before giving it to your child.

Omega-3 Fatty Acids Omega-3 fatty acids have anti-inflammatory properties that can help reduce asthma symptoms. Including omega-3-rich foods in your child's diet, such as fatty fish (salmon, mackerel, sardines), flaxseeds, and chia seeds, can support respiratory health. Omega-3 supplements are also available, but it's best to consult with a healthcare professional before starting any new supplement.

Lifestyle Changes Making certain lifestyle changes can help manage asthma and reduce the frequency and severity of asthma attacks. These include:

Identifying Triggers: Identifying and avoiding asthma triggers, such as pollen, dust mites, pet dander, smoke, and strong odors, can help reduce asthma symptoms. Keeping a diary of asthma attacks and potential triggers can be helpful.

Regular Exercise: Regular physical activity can improve lung function and overall health. Encourage your child to engage in activities like swimming, walking, or cycling. Always ensure they have their inhaler on hand during exercise.

Healthy Diet: A balanced diet rich in fruits, vegetables, whole grains, and lean proteins can support overall health and reduce inflammation. Avoiding processed foods, additives, and allergens can also help manage asthma symptoms.

4

DIGESTIVE PROBLEMS

Constipation

Constipation in children can cause discomfort, pain, and a general sense of unease. It's often the result of a diet low in fiber, inadequate fluid intake, or a lack of physical activity. Natural remedies can help relieve constipation and promote regular bowel movements.

Prune Juice Prune juice is a well-known natural remedy for constipation. Prunes are rich in fiber and contain sorbitol, a natural laxative that helps soften the stool. To use prune juice for constipation, start with a small amount, such as 2-4 ounces, and see how your child responds. If needed, you can gradually increase the amount. For younger children, you can dilute the prune juice with water to make it more palatable. Offer it in the morning to help stimulate bowel movements throughout the day.

High-Fiber Foods A diet high in fiber is essential for preventing and treating constipation. Fiber adds bulk to the stool and helps it pass more easily through the intestines. Incorporate high-fiber foods into your child's diet, such as:

- Fruits: Apples (with skin), pears, berries, and oranges

- Vegetables: Broccoli, carrots, peas, and spinach

- Whole grains: Oatmeal, whole wheat bread, brown rice, and quinoa

- Legumes: Beans, lentils, and chickpeas

Encourage your child to drink plenty of water throughout the day, as fiber works best when combined with adequate hydration.

Physical Activity Regular physical activity can help stimulate digestion and promote regular bowel movements. Encourage your child to engage in activities like walking, playing outside, or riding a bike. Aim for at least 30 minutes of physical activity each day to help keep their digestive system functioning properly.

Hydration Adequate hydration is crucial for preventing constipation. Encourage your child to drink plenty of fluids, especially water, throughout the day. Herbal teas and clear broths can also help keep them hydrated.

Aloe Vera Juice Aloe vera juice can help relieve constipation by acting as a natural laxative. Ensure you use a product specifically labeled for internal use, as some aloe vera products are meant for external use only. Start with a small amount and monitor your child's response.

Massage A gentle abdominal massage can help stimulate bowel movements and relieve constipation. Using a bit of warm oil (such as olive or coconut oil), gently massage your child's abdomen in a clockwise direction for a few minutes. This can help encourage the movement of stool through the intestines.

Indigestion

Indigestion can cause discomfort, bloating, and pain in children. It can be triggered by overeating, eating too quickly, or consuming certain foods. Natural remedies can help soothe the digestive system and relieve symptoms.

Fennel Seeds Fennel seeds have carminative properties that can help reduce bloating and indigestion. Chewing a small amount of fennel seeds after meals can help improve digestion and alleviate symptoms. For younger children, you can make fennel tea by steeping a teaspoon of crushed fennel seeds in a cup of hot water for 10 minutes. Strain and let it cool before giving it to your child.

Ginger Tea Ginger is known for its digestive benefits and can help relieve nausea and indigestion. To make ginger tea, slice a small piece of fresh ginger and simmer it in a cup of water for 10-15 minutes. Strain and let it cool before giving it to your child. Ginger tea can help soothe the stomach and improve digestion.

Peppermint Tea Peppermint tea can help relax the muscles of the digestive tract and alleviate symptoms of indigestion. Steep one teaspoon of dried peppermint leaves in a cup of hot water for 5-10 minutes. Strain and let it cool before giving it to your child. Peppermint tea can help reduce bloating, gas, and stomach pain.

Apple Cider Vinegar Apple cider vinegar can help balance stomach acid and improve digestion. Mix one teaspoon of apple cider vinegar with a cup of warm water and give it to your child before meals. This can help stimulate digestion and prevent indigestion.

Chamomile Tea Chamomile tea has soothing and anti-inflammatory properties that can help relieve indigestion. Steep one teaspoon of dried chamomile flowers in a cup of hot water for 5-10 minutes. Strain and let it cool before giving it to your child. Chamomile tea can help calm the digestive system and reduce discomfort.

Probiotics Probiotics can help restore the balance of good bacteria in the gut and improve digestion. Foods rich in probiotics, such as yogurt, kefir, and fermented vegetables, can be beneficial for children with indigestion. Probiotic supplements are also available, but it's best to consult with a healthcare professional before starting any new supplement.

Dietary Adjustments Making certain dietary adjustments can help prevent and relieve indigestion. Encourage your child to eat smaller, more frequent meals instead of large meals. Avoid foods that are known to trigger indigestion, such as spicy, fatty, or fried foods. Encourage your child to eat slowly and chew their food thoroughly.

Colic

Colic is a common condition in infants characterized by prolonged periods of crying and discomfort, often due to gas or digestive issues. Natural remedies can help soothe colic and provide relief for both the baby and the parents.

Warm Baths A warm bath can help relax your baby and relieve colic symptoms. Fill a bathtub with warm water (not too hot) and gently place your baby in the bath. The warmth of the water can help soothe their muscles and reduce discomfort. You can also add a few drops of lavender or chamomile essential oil to the bathwater to enhance the calming effect.

Gentle Tummy Massage A gentle tummy massage can help stimulate digestion and relieve gas, providing relief from colic. Using a bit of warm oil (such as olive or coconut oil), gently massage your baby's abdomen in a clockwise direction for a few minutes. This can help move gas through the intestines and reduce discomfort. Be gentle and use soft, circular motions.

Bicycle Legs Bicycle legs is a simple exercise that can help relieve gas and colic symptoms. Lay your baby on their back and gently move their legs in a bicycling motion, bringing one knee up to their chest while extending the other leg. This motion can help release trapped gas and provide relief from discomfort.

Gripe Water Gripe water is a traditional remedy for colic that contains a mixture of herbs and water. It can help soothe the digestive system and relieve gas. Look for a gripe water product that is free from alcohol and artificial additives. Follow the dosage instructions on the packaging, and consult with a healthcare professional before giving it to your baby.

Chamomile Tea Chamomile tea can help soothe the digestive system and reduce colic symptoms. For infants, prepare a weak chamomile tea by steeping half a teaspoon of dried chamomile flowers in a cup of hot water for 5 minutes. Strain and let it cool completely. Give your baby a few teaspoons of the tea using a dropper or spoon. Chamomile can help calm the digestive system and promote relaxation.

Babywearing Wearing your baby in a sling or carrier can help provide comfort and reduce colic symptoms. The gentle movement and close contact with the parent can help soothe the baby and reduce crying. Babywearing can also help promote bonding and provide a sense of security for the baby.

Probiotics Probiotics can help improve digestion and reduce colic symptoms by restoring the balance of good bacteria in the gut. Probiotic drops specifically formulated for infants are available and can be added to breast milk or formula. Consult with a healthcare professional before starting any new supplement.

Dietary Adjustments for Breastfeeding Mothers If you are breastfeeding, certain foods in your diet may contribute to your baby's colic symptoms. Common culprits include dairy, caffeine, spicy foods, and certain vegetables like broccoli and cabbage. Keeping a food diary and noting any changes in your baby's symptoms can help identify potential triggers. Consult with a healthcare professional before making significant dietary changes.

5

SLEEP ISSUES

Insomnia

Insomnia can be a distressing issue for children and parents alike, leading to fatigue, irritability, and poor concentration. Establishing healthy sleep habits and using natural remedies can help promote better sleep.

Chamomile Tea Chamomile tea is well-known for its calming and soothing properties. It can help relax the mind and body, making it easier for children to fall asleep. To prepare chamomile tea, steep one teaspoon of dried chamomile flowers in a cup of hot water for 5-10 minutes. Strain and let it cool before giving it to your child. Adding a bit of honey can improve the taste (for children over one year old). Give the tea to your child about 30 minutes before bedtime to help them wind down.

Bedtime Routine Establishing a consistent bedtime routine is crucial for promoting healthy sleep habits. A predictable routine helps signal to your child's body that it is time to sleep. Here are some steps to include in a bedtime routine:

- **Consistent Bedtime**: Set a regular bedtime and stick to it every night, even on weekends.

- **Relaxing Activities**: Include calming activities such as reading a book, taking a warm bath, or listening to soft music.

- **Dim the Lights**: Lower the lighting in your home about an hour before bedtime to help signal to your child's body that it is time to wind down.

- **Limit Screen Time**: Avoid screens (TV, tablets, phones) at least an hour before bedtime, as the blue light can interfere with the production of melatonin, the sleep hormone.

- **Comfortable Sleep Environment**: Ensure your child's bedroom is conducive to sleep by keeping it cool, quiet, and dark. Use blackout curtains if necessary to block out light.

Essential Oils Lavender essential oil has calming properties that can help promote relaxation and sleep. You can add a few drops of lavender oil to a diffuser in your child's room or dilute it with a carrier oil and apply it to their wrists or temples before bed. Other essential oils that can aid sleep include chamomile and sandalwood.

White Noise White noise can help block out background noises and create a soothing environment for sleep. You can use a white noise machine or a fan to produce a steady, calming sound. This can be particularly helpful for children who are sensitive to noise.

Nightmares

Nightmares can disrupt sleep and cause fear and anxiety in children. Natural remedies and comforting bedtime practices can help reduce the frequency of nightmares and provide reassurance.

Lavender Pillow Spray Lavender has calming and soothing properties that can help create a sense of security and relaxation. To make a lavender pillow spray, mix a few drops of lavender essential oil with water in a spray bottle. Lightly mist your child's pillow and bedding before bedtime. The scent of lavender can help calm their mind and reduce the likelihood of nightmares.

Calming Bedtime Stories Reading calming and positive bedtime stories can help create a peaceful atmosphere before sleep. Choose stories that are gentle and have happy endings. Avoid books with scary or intense themes that might trigger nightmares. Reading together can also provide a sense of security and comfort for your child.

Nightlight A soft nightlight can help alleviate fear of the dark and provide a sense of security. Choose a nightlight with a gentle, warm glow rather than a bright, harsh light. This can help your child feel more comfortable and safe in their room.

Dream Catchers Some children find comfort in the idea of dream catchers, which are believed to trap bad dreams and allow good dreams to pass through. Hanging a dream catcher above your child's bed can provide a sense of protection and reduce anxiety about nightmares.

Reassurance and Comfort If your child wakes up from a nightmare, provide reassurance and comfort. Gently remind them that it was just a dream and that they are safe. Stay with them until they feel calm and ready to go back to sleep. Consistent reassurance can help reduce anxiety about nightmares over time.

Restlessness

Restlessness can make it difficult for children to fall asleep and stay asleep. Addressing the underlying causes and using natural remedies can help promote more restful sleep.

Magnesium-Rich Foods Magnesium is a mineral that plays a crucial role in promoting relaxation and sleep. Including magnesium-rich foods in your child's diet can help reduce restlessness. Some good sources of magnesium include:

- Leafy greens (spinach, kale)

- Nuts and seeds (almonds, pumpkin seeds)

- Whole grains (brown rice, oatmeal)

- Legumes (black beans, lentils)

- Bananas

You can also consider giving your child a magnesium supplement, but it's best to consult with a healthcare professional before starting any new supplement.

Warm Milk Warm milk is a traditional remedy for promoting sleep. It contains tryptophan, an amino acid that can help induce sleep. Warm up a cup of milk and offer it to your child about 30 minutes before bedtime. Adding a bit of honey or a pinch of cinnamon can enhance the taste and calming effects.

Epsom Salt Bath An Epsom salt bath can help relax the muscles and promote a sense of calm. Epsom salts are rich in magnesium, which can be absorbed through the skin. Add a cup of Epsom salts to a warm bath and let your child soak for 15-20 minutes before bedtime. This can help reduce restlessness and prepare their body for sleep.

Calming Bedtime Rituals Incorporate calming rituals into your child's bedtime routine to help them unwind. These can include:

- **Gentle Massage**: A gentle massage with a bit of lavender or chamomile oil can help relax the muscles and calm the mind.

- **Breathing Exercises**: Teach your child simple breathing exercises to help them relax. Have them take slow, deep breaths in through their nose and out through their mouth.

- **Meditation or Guided Imagery**: Listening to a guided meditation or practicing guided imagery can help your child relax and prepare for sleep. There are many child-friendly meditation apps and recordings available.

Consistency and Routine Maintaining a consistent bedtime routine is crucial for promoting restful sleep. Stick to the same routine every night, even on weekends, to help regulate your child's internal clock. Consistency can help reduce restlessness and make it easier for your child to fall asleep and stay asleep.

Limiting Stimulants Avoid giving your child stimulants such as caffeine or sugar in the evening. These can interfere with their ability to fall asleep and stay asleep. Encourage healthy eating habits and limit sugary snacks and drinks, especially in the hours leading up to bedtime.

6

BOOSTING IMMUNITY

A strong immune system is essential for children to ward off infections and stay healthy. While genetics play a role in immune function, lifestyle choices can significantly influence the immune system's strength and effectiveness. This chapter explores natural ways to boost immunity in children, focusing on diet, herbal supplements, and lifestyle changes.

Nutrient-Rich Diet

A balanced, nutrient-rich diet is the foundation of a strong immune system. Ensuring that children consume a variety of healthy foods helps provide the essential vitamins, minerals, and antioxidants needed for optimal immune function.

Fruits and Vegetables Fruits and vegetables are packed with vitamins, minerals, and antioxidants that support the immune system. Encourage your child to eat a colorful variety of fruits and vegetables to ensure they get a broad spectrum of nutrients.

- **Vitamin C**: Citrus fruits (oranges, lemons, grapefruits), strawberries, kiwi, bell peppers, and broccoli are high in vitamin C, which boosts the immune system by promoting the production of white blood cells.

- **Beta-Carotene**: Carrots, sweet potatoes, and leafy greens like spinach and kale are rich in beta-carotene, which the body converts into vitamin A. Vitamin A is crucial for maintaining the integrity of the skin and mucous membranes, which are the body's first line of defense against pathogens.

- **Antioxidants**: Berries (blueberries, raspberries, blackberries) are high in antioxidants, which help protect the body from oxidative stress and support immune function.

Incorporate these nutrient-dense foods into meals and snacks to boost your child's immune health. Smoothies, salads, vegetable soups, and fruit platters are great ways to include a variety of fruits and vegetables in their diet.

Probiotic Foods Probiotics are beneficial bacteria that support gut health, which is closely linked to immune function. A healthy gut microbiome helps the body fend off harmful pathogens and enhances the immune response.

- **Yogurt**: Yogurt with live and active cultures is an excellent source of probiotics. Choose plain, unsweetened yogurt and add fresh fruit for natural sweetness.

- **Kefir**: Kefir is a fermented milk drink that contains a higher concentration of probiotics than yogurt. It can be enjoyed on its own or added to smoothies.

- **Fermented Foods**: Foods like sauerkraut, kimchi, and pickles (naturally fermented) are rich in probiotics. These can be added to meals as side dishes or snacks.

- **Miso**: Miso, a fermented soybean paste, can be used to make soups and sauces that are both nutritious and probiotic-rich.

Encouraging your child to consume probiotic foods regularly can help maintain a healthy gut microbiome and support their overall immune health.

Hydration Adequate hydration is also crucial for a healthy immune system. Water helps transport nutrients to cells and remove toxins from the body. Encourage your child to drink plenty of water throughout the day, and offer hydrating foods like fruits and vegetables with high water content.

Herbal Supplements

Herbal supplements can provide additional support for the immune system, especially during times of increased susceptibility to illness. Two well-known immune-boosting herbs are echinacea and elderberry.

Echinacea Echinacea is a herb that has been traditionally used to enhance immune function and fight infections. It is believed to stimulate the production of white blood cells, which are essential for combating pathogens.

- **Echinacea Tea**: Echinacea tea can be made by steeping dried echinacea roots or leaves in hot water for 5-10 minutes. Let it cool before giving it to your child. A bit of honey can be added for sweetness (for children over one year old).

- **Echinacea Supplements**: Echinacea is also available in the form of capsules, tinctures, and syrups. Follow the dosage instructions on the product and consult with a healthcare professional before starting any new supplement, especially for young children.

Elderberry Syrup Elderberry is rich in antioxidants and has antiviral properties that can help boost the immune system and reduce the duration and severity of colds and flu.

- **Elderberry Syrup**: Elderberry syrup can be purchased at health food stores or made at home. To make elderberry syrup, simmer fresh or dried elderberries with water and a bit of honey or sugar until it thickens into a syrup. Give your child a teaspoon of elderberry syrup daily during cold and flu season.

- **Elderberry Gummies**: Elderberry gummies are a child-friendly way to consume elderberry. These can be purchased or made at home using elderberry syrup, gelatin, and molds.

Astragalus Astragalus is a lesser-known herb that can enhance immune function and increase resistance to infections.

- **Astragalus Tea**: Astragalus root can be simmered in water to make a tea. Let it cool before giving it to your child. This herb is often used in Traditional Chinese Medicine to support the immune system.

- **Astragalus Supplements**: Astragalus is available in capsules, tinctures, and powders. As with any supplement, consult with a healthcare professional before use.

Lifestyle Changes

Healthy lifestyle habits are essential for maintaining a robust immune system. Regular exercise, adequate sleep, and stress management are key components of a healthy lifestyle.

Regular Exercise Physical activity is important for overall health and can help boost the immune system. Exercise improves circulation, which allows immune cells to move through the body more effectively.

- **Outdoor Play**: Encourage your child to play outside, where they can run, jump, and explore. Activities like biking, hiking, and playing sports provide physical exercise and fresh air.

- **Family Activities**: Engage in physical activities as a family, such as walking, swimming, or playing games in the park. This not only promotes physical health but also strengthens family bonds.

- **Active Play**: Encourage activities that get your child moving, such as dancing, jumping rope, or playing on playground equipment.

Adequate Sleep Sleep is crucial for a healthy immune system. During sleep, the body produces cytokines, which are proteins that help fight infections and inflammation.

- **Consistent Sleep Schedule**: Establish a regular sleep schedule for your child, with consistent bedtimes and wake-up times, even on weekends.

- **Sleep Environment**: Create a comfortable sleep environment by keeping the room cool, dark, and quiet. A comfortable mattress and bedding can also enhance sleep quality.

- **Bedtime Routine**: Follow a calming bedtime routine to help your child wind down. This can include activities like reading a book, taking a warm bath, or listening to soft music.

Stress Management Chronic stress can weaken the immune system and make the body more susceptible to illness. Teaching children healthy ways to manage stress is important for their overall well-being.

- **Mindfulness and Relaxation**: Teach your child simple mindfulness and relaxation techniques, such as deep breathing, progressive muscle relaxation, or guided imagery. These practices can help reduce stress and promote a sense of calm.

- **Physical Activity**: Physical activity can also help reduce stress. Encourage your child to engage in activities they enjoy, whether it's playing sports, dancing, or riding a bike.

- **Creative Outlets**: Encourage creative activities like drawing, painting, or playing a musical instrument as a way for your child to express themselves and manage stress.

- **Quality Time**: Spend quality time with your child, providing emotional support and creating a safe space for them to talk about their feelings and concerns.

Hygiene Practices Good hygiene practices are essential for preventing infections and supporting the immune system.

- **Hand Washing**: Teach your child to wash their hands regularly with soap and water, especially before eating, after using the bathroom, and after playing outside. Proper hand washing can help prevent the spread of germs.

- **Cough and Sneeze Etiquette**: Encourage your child to cover their mouth and nose with a tissue or their elbow when coughing or sneezing. Dispose of tissues properly and wash hands afterward.

- **Avoiding Sick Individuals**: If possible, keep your child away from individuals who are sick to reduce the risk of infection.

Teach your child to avoid close contact and to practice good hygiene around others.

7

BEHAVIORAL AND EMOTIONAL HEALTH

Children's behavioral and emotional health is just as important as their physical health. It can impact their ability to learn, interact with others, and overall well-being. This chapter explores natural ways to support and enhance behavioral and emotional health, focusing on managing anxiety, hyperactivity, and mood swings.

Anxiety

Anxiety in children can manifest as excessive worry, fear, or nervousness. It can affect their daily activities and overall quality of life. Natural remedies and techniques can help manage anxiety and promote a sense of calm.

Herbal Teas (Lemon Balm, Valerian Root) Herbal teas can be an effective and gentle way to alleviate anxiety in children.

- **Lemon Balm Tea**: Lemon balm is known for its calming effects and can help reduce anxiety and promote relaxation. To make lemon balm tea, steep one teaspoon of dried lemon balm leaves in a cup of hot water for 5-10 minutes. Strain and let it cool before giving it to your child. Adding a bit of honey can enhance the flavor (for children over one year old).

- **Valerian Root Tea**: Valerian root is another herb known for its calming properties. However, it has a strong taste, so it might not be as appealing to children. To make valerian root tea, steep one teaspoon of dried valerian root in a cup of hot water for 10-15 minutes. Strain and let it cool before giving it to your child. Valerian root can help reduce anxiety and promote better sleep.

Relaxation Techniques Teaching children relaxation techniques can help them manage anxiety and stress more effectively.

- **Deep Breathing**: Deep breathing exercises can help calm the nervous system and reduce anxiety. Teach your child to take slow, deep breaths in through their nose, hold for a few seconds, and then exhale slowly through their mouth. Practicing deep breathing regularly can help them use this technique when they feel anxious.

- **Progressive Muscle Relaxation**: This technique involves tensing and then relaxing different muscle groups in the body. Start with the feet and work up to the head, instructing your child to tense each muscle group for a few seconds before relaxing. This can help release physical tension and promote relaxation.

- **Mindfulness and Meditation**: Mindfulness exercises and meditation can help children focus on the present moment and reduce anxiety. Simple practices like mindful breathing, guided imagery, or listening to calming music can be effective. There are many child-friendly meditation apps and recordings available to help guide these practices.

Routine and Structure Establishing a predictable routine and structure can help reduce anxiety by providing a sense of stability and security. Consistent daily routines, such as regular meal times, homework time, and bedtime, can help children feel more in control and less anxious.

Physical Activity Regular physical activity can help reduce anxiety by releasing endorphins, the body's natural stress-relievers. Encourage your child to engage in activities they enjoy, such as playing sports, dancing, or simply playing outside. Physical activity can also provide a healthy outlet for releasing pent-up energy and stress.

Creative Outlets Creative activities like drawing, painting, writing, or playing music can help children express their feelings and manage anxiety. Encourage your child to engage in creative activities that they enjoy and provide opportunities for them to explore different forms of self-expression.

Hyperactivity

Hyperactivity in children can manifest as restlessness, impulsiveness, and difficulty focusing. It can affect their ability to concentrate and perform well in school. Natural remedies and techniques can help manage hyperactivity and improve focus.

Omega-3 Fatty Acids Omega-3 fatty acids are essential for brain health and can help improve attention and reduce hyperactivity in children. Foods rich in omega-3s include:

- **Fatty Fish**: Salmon, mackerel, sardines, and trout are excellent sources of omega-3 fatty acids. Try to include these fish in your child's diet at least twice a week.

- **Flaxseeds and Chia Seeds**: These seeds are rich in omega-3s and can be added to smoothies, yogurt, or oatmeal.

- **Walnuts**: Walnuts are another good source of omega-3s and can be included in snacks or meals.

- **Omega-3 Supplements**: If it's difficult to include enough omega-3-rich foods in your child's diet, consider giving them an omega-3 supplement. Consult with a healthcare professional before starting any new supplement.

Mindfulness Exercises Mindfulness exercises can help children improve their focus and self-regulation, reducing hyperactivity.

- **Mindful Breathing**: Teach your child to focus on their breath, taking slow, deep breaths in and out. Encourage them to notice how their body feels with each breath. This practice can help them become more aware of their body and mind, promoting a sense of calm.

- **Body Scan**: Guide your child through a body scan meditation, where they focus on different parts of their body, starting from their toes and moving up to their head. This can help them become more aware of physical sensations and promote relaxation.

- **Mindful Movement**: Activities like yoga or tai chi can combine physical movement with mindfulness, helping children improve their focus and self-regulation. There are many child-friendly yoga videos and classes available to guide these practices.

Dietary Adjustments Certain dietary adjustments can help manage hyperactivity in children.

- **Reduce Sugar and Processed Foods**: High sugar intake and processed foods can contribute to hyperactivity. Limit sugary snacks and drinks and focus on providing whole, nutrient-dense foods.

- **Balanced Meals**: Ensure your child's meals are balanced and include a mix of protein, healthy fats, and complex carbohydrates. This can help maintain stable blood sugar levels and reduce hyperactivity.

- **Hydration**: Keeping your child well-hydrated is important for overall health and can help improve concentration. Encourage your child to drink plenty of water throughout the day.

Physical Activity Regular physical activity can help manage hyperactivity by providing an outlet for excess energy. Encourage your child to engage in physical activities they enjoy, such as sports, dancing, or playing outside. Aim for at least 60 minutes of physical activity each day.

Mood Swings

Mood swings in children can be challenging to manage and can affect their overall well-being and interactions with others. Natural remedies and lifestyle changes can help stabilize mood and promote emotional balance.

Balanced Diet A balanced diet is essential for maintaining stable mood and energy levels. Certain nutrients play a crucial role in brain health and mood regulation.

- **Complex Carbohydrates**: Foods like whole grains, fruits, and vegetables provide a steady source of energy and help maintain stable blood sugar levels, reducing mood swings.

- **Protein**: Protein-rich foods like lean meats, fish, eggs, beans, and nuts provide essential amino acids that support neurotransmitter production, which can affect mood.

- **Healthy Fats**: Omega-3 fatty acids, found in fatty fish, flaxseeds, chia seeds, and walnuts, support brain health and can help stabilize mood.

- **Vitamins and Minerals**: Ensure your child gets enough vitamins and minerals, particularly vitamin B6, magnesium, and zinc, which play a role in mood regulation. Foods rich in these nutrients include leafy greens, nuts, seeds, and whole grains.

Routine and Structure Establishing a consistent routine and structure can help stabilize mood by providing a sense of predictability and security.

- **Consistent Daily Schedule**: Maintain a regular schedule for meals, homework, playtime, and bedtime. Consistency can help children feel more secure and reduce mood swings.

- **Bedtime Routine**: A calming bedtime routine can help promote better sleep, which is essential for mood regulation. Include activities like reading a book, taking a warm bath, or listening to soft music.

- **Morning Routine**: Starting the day with a positive morning routine can set the tone for the rest of the day. Encourage activities like a healthy breakfast, gentle stretching, or a few minutes of mindfulness or deep breathing.

Physical Activity Regular physical activity is important for overall well-being and can help stabilize mood. Encourage your child to engage in physical activities they enjoy, such as sports, dancing, or playing outside. Physical activity can help release endorphins, which are natural mood-boosters.

Emotional Expression and Support Providing opportunities for emotional expression and support can help children manage mood swings and develop emotional resilience.

- **Creative Outlets**: Encourage your child to express their emotions through creative activities like drawing, painting, writing, or playing music. Creative expression can be a healthy way to process and release emotions.

- **Open Communication**: Create a safe and supportive environment for your child to talk about their feelings and concerns. Listen actively and validate their emotions, helping them feel understood and supported.

- **Emotional Regulation Skills**: Teach your child skills for managing their emotions, such as deep breathing, progressive muscle relaxation, or mindfulness exercises. These techniques can help them cope with mood swings and develop emotional resilience.

8

PREVENTIVE CARE

Preventive care is essential for maintaining children's health and preventing illnesses. By incorporating regular check-ups, vaccinations, and good hygiene practices into your routine, you can help ensure your child's well-being. This chapter explores the importance of these preventive measures and how to complement them with natural approaches.

Regular Check-ups

Regular check-ups with a pediatrician are crucial for monitoring your child's growth and development, identifying potential health issues early, and ensuring they receive necessary vaccinations and screenings.

Importance of Pediatric Visits Pediatric visits play a vital role in preventive care. Here's why regular check-ups are essential:

- **Monitoring Growth and Development**: Regular visits allow pediatricians to track your child's growth and development, ensuring they are meeting appropriate milestones. They can identify any potential delays or issues early and provide guidance or referrals for further evaluation if needed.

- **Early Detection of Health Issues**: Pediatricians can detect early signs of health problems through physical exams, screenings, and routine tests. Early detection allows for timely intervention and treatment, which can prevent complications and improve outcomes.

- **Vaccinations**: Vaccinations are a critical part of preventive care, protecting children from serious and potentially life-threatening diseases. Pediatricians ensure that children receive vaccinations on schedule, providing immunity against various illnesses.

- **Health Education**: Pediatricians provide valuable information and advice on nutrition, physical activity, sleep, safety, and overall wellness. They can address any concerns or questions parents may have and offer guidance on promoting healthy habits.

- **Building a Trusting Relationship**: Regular visits help build a trusting relationship between the child, parents, and the pediatrician. This relationship is important for effective communication, addressing health concerns, and providing comprehensive care.

Frequency of Check-ups The American Academy of Pediatrics (AAP) recommends the following schedule for well-child visits:

- Newborn (within the first week)

- 1 month

- 2 months

- 4 months

- 6 months

- 9 months

- 12 months

- 15 months

- 18 months

- 24 months

- 30 months

- Annually from 3 years onward

Follow your pediatrician's recommendations for check-up frequency, as they may vary based on your child's individual needs.

Vaccinations

Vaccinations are a cornerstone of preventive care, providing protection against a range of infectious diseases. Complementing vaccinations with natural immunity boosters can further support your child's immune system.

Complementing with Natural Immunity Boosters While vaccinations are crucial for preventing specific diseases, natural immunity boosters can enhance overall immune function and help protect against other infections. Here are some natural ways to support your child's immune system:

- **Nutrient-Rich Diet**: A balanced diet rich in fruits, vegetables, whole grains, lean proteins, and healthy fats provides essential vitamins and minerals that support immune health. Include foods high in vitamin C, vitamin A, zinc, and antioxidants to boost immunity.

- **Probiotic Foods**: Probiotics support gut health, which is closely linked to immune function. Include probiotic-rich foods like yogurt, kefir, sauerkraut, and kimchi in your child's diet.

- **Herbal Supplements**: Herbs like echinacea and elderberry can help boost the immune system. Echinacea is believed to stimulate white blood cell production, while elderberry has antiviral properties. Consult with a healthcare professional before giving any herbal supplements to your child.

- **Adequate Sleep**: Sleep is essential for immune function. Ensure your child gets enough sleep each night according to their age group. Establish a consistent bedtime routine and create a sleep-friendly environment.

- **Regular Exercise**: Physical activity promotes overall health and strengthens the immune system. Encourage your child to engage in regular physical activities they enjoy, such as playing outside, riding a bike, or participating in sports.

- **Hydration**: Proper hydration is important for maintaining a healthy immune system. Encourage your child to drink plenty of water throughout the day and limit sugary drinks.

Hygiene Practices

Good hygiene practices are fundamental in preventing the spread of infections and maintaining overall health. Teaching children proper hygiene habits can help protect them and those around them.

Hand Washing Hand washing is one of the most effective ways to prevent the spread of germs. Teach your child the importance of washing their hands regularly, especially:

- Before eating

- After using the bathroom

- After playing outside

- After coughing, sneezing, or blowing their nose

- After touching animals or pets

Proper Hand Washing Technique:

1. Wet hands with clean, running water (warm or cold).

2. Apply soap and lather well, covering all surfaces of the hands, including the backs, between the fingers, and under the nails.

3. Scrub hands for at least 20 seconds. A good guideline is to sing the "Happy Birthday" song twice.

4. Rinse hands thoroughly under clean, running water.

5. Dry hands using a clean towel or air dry them.

Hand Sanitizer: When soap and water are not available, use a hand sanitizer with at least 60% alcohol. Apply enough sanitizer to cover all surfaces of the hands and rub them together until dry.

Proper Sanitation Proper sanitation practices are essential for maintaining a clean and healthy environment. Here are some tips for ensuring proper sanitation at home:

- **Regular Cleaning**: Clean and disinfect frequently-touched surfaces, such as doorknobs, light switches, remote controls, and toys. Use disinfectant wipes or sprays to kill germs.

- **Safe Food Handling**: Practice safe food handling by washing hands before and after handling food, washing fruits and vegetables, cooking meat thoroughly, and avoiding cross-contamination.

- **Toothbrush Hygiene**: Replace toothbrushes every three to four months or sooner if the bristles become frayed. Store toothbrushes in an upright position and allow them to air dry.

- **Bathing and Personal Hygiene**: Encourage regular bathing and personal hygiene practices, such as brushing teeth twice a day, washing hair, and keeping nails trimmed and clean.

Cough and Sneeze Etiquette Teach your child proper cough and sneeze etiquette to prevent the spread of germs:

- **Covering Mouth and Nose**: Encourage your child to cover their mouth and nose with a tissue when coughing or sneezing. If a tissue is not available, they should use the inside of their elbow.

- **Disposing of Tissues**: Ensure that used tissues are disposed of in the trash and not left lying around.

- **Hand Washing**: Remind your child to wash their hands immediately after coughing, sneezing, or blowing their nose.

Safe Play Promote safe play practices to reduce the risk of injury and infection:

- **Safe Toys**: Choose age-appropriate toys that are free from sharp edges or small parts that can be swallowed. Regularly clean and disinfect toys, especially those that are shared with other children.

- **Outdoor Safety**: Ensure that outdoor play areas are safe and free from hazards. Supervise outdoor play and encourage your child to wear appropriate protective gear, such as helmets and knee pads, when necessary.

- **Pet Hygiene**: Teach your child how to safely interact with pets, including washing hands after handling animals and keeping pet areas clean.

9

FIRST AID AND SAFETY

First aid and safety measures are crucial for ensuring the well-being of children. Accidents and injuries can happen at any time, and being prepared with the right knowledge and supplies can make all the difference. This chapter covers the essentials of a basic first aid kit, natural remedies for minor injuries, and important safety tips for childproofing the home and educating kids about safety.

Basic First Aid Kit

Having a well-stocked first aid kit at home is essential for handling minor injuries and emergencies. Here are the essential items that should be included in a basic first aid kit:

Essential Items to Have at Home

1. **Adhesive Bandages (Various Sizes)**: For covering minor cuts, blisters, and abrasions.

2. **Sterile Gauze Pads and Adhesive Tape**: For larger cuts and wounds that require more coverage and protection.

3. **Antiseptic Wipes**: For cleaning wounds and preventing infection.

4. **Antibiotic Ointment**: To apply on cuts and abrasions to prevent infection and promote healing.

5. **Hydrogen Peroxide**: For cleaning wounds and preventing infection.

6. **Tweezers**: For removing splinters, ticks, or debris from wounds.

7. **Scissors**: For cutting tape, gauze, or clothing if needed.

8. **Instant Cold Packs**: For reducing swelling and pain from sprains, strains, or insect bites.

9. **Thermometer**: For checking body temperature during illness.

10. **Hydrocortisone Cream**: For relieving itching and inflammation from insect bites, rashes, or allergic reactions.

11. **Pain Relievers (Acetaminophen or Ibuprofen)**: For reducing pain and fever. Ensure appropriate dosages for children.

12. **Digital Thermometer**: For checking body temperature accurately.

13. **Saline Solution**: For cleaning wounds or flushing out eyes.

14. **Elastic Bandage**: For wrapping sprains or strains.

15. **Alcohol Swabs**: For disinfecting skin and tools.

16. **Sterile Gloves**: For protecting yourself and the injured person while providing first aid.

17. **First Aid Manual**: For reference in case of emergency.

Keep your first aid kit in an easily accessible location and ensure that all family members know where it is stored. Regularly check and replenish the supplies to ensure they are up to date and ready for use.

Natural Remedies for Minor Injuries

Natural remedies can be effective for treating minor injuries and promoting healing. Here are some common natural remedies for burns and bruises:

Aloe Vera for Burns Aloe vera is well-known for its soothing and healing properties, making it an excellent remedy for minor burns.

- **Application**: For minor burns, cool the affected area under running water for several minutes. After cooling, apply a thin layer of pure aloe vera gel directly to the burn. Aloe vera can help reduce pain, inflammation, and promote faster healing. Reapply the gel several times a day as needed.

- **Aloe Vera Gel**: Ensure you use 100% pure aloe vera gel without any added chemicals or fragrances. Aloe vera plants are easy to grow at home, and having one can provide a fresh source of gel for immediate use.

Arnica for Bruises Arnica is a natural remedy that can help reduce swelling, pain, and discoloration associated with bruises.

- **Application**: Apply arnica gel or cream to the bruised area as soon as possible after the injury occurs. Reapply several times a day to help reduce inflammation and speed up the healing process.

- **Arnica Gel or Cream**: Arnica is available in various forms, including gels, creams, and ointments. Ensure the product is intended for topical use and follow the instructions on the packaging.

Honey for Cuts and Scrapes Honey has natural antibacterial and anti-inflammatory properties, making it effective for treating minor cuts and scrapes.

- **Application**: Clean the wound with water and mild soap. Apply a thin layer of raw honey to the wound and cover it with a sterile bandage. Honey helps prevent infection and promotes faster healing.

- **Raw Honey**: Use raw, unpasteurized honey for its medicinal properties. Manuka honey is particularly known for its potent antibacterial effects.

Tea Tree Oil for Insect Bites Tea tree oil has antiseptic and anti-inflammatory properties, making it effective for treating insect bites.

- **Application**: Dilute a few drops of tea tree oil with a carrier oil, such as coconut or olive oil, and apply it to the insect bite. This can help reduce itching, swelling, and prevent infection.

- **Tea Tree Oil**: Ensure the tea tree oil is pure and of high quality. Always dilute essential oils before applying them to the skin.

Witch Hazel for Rashes Witch hazel is a natural astringent that can help soothe skin irritation and reduce inflammation.

- **Application**: Apply witch hazel to a cotton ball or pad and gently dab it onto the affected area. This can help relieve itching and inflammation associated with rashes.

- **Witch Hazel**: Use pure witch hazel extract without added alcohol or fragrances for the best results.

Safety Tips

Creating a safe environment for children involves taking preventive measures and educating them about safety. Here are some essential safety tips for childproofing the home and educating kids on safety:

Childproofing the Home

1. **Secure Furniture and Appliances**: Use brackets or straps to secure heavy furniture, such as bookshelves and dressers, to the wall to prevent tipping. Secure large appliances, such as TVs and ovens, to prevent accidents.

2. **Use Safety Gates**: Install safety gates at the top and bottom of stairs to prevent falls. Use gates to block off areas that are not child-friendly, such as kitchens or bathrooms.

3. **Cover Electrical Outlets**: Use outlet covers or safety plugs to prevent children from inserting objects into electrical outlets.

4. **Keep Hazardous Materials Out of Reach**: Store cleaning supplies, medications, and other hazardous materials in locked cabinets or out of reach of children.

5. **Use Corner Guards**: Place corner guards on sharp edges of furniture, such as coffee tables and countertops, to prevent injuries.

6. **Install Window Guards**: Install window guards or stops to prevent children from falling out of windows. Ensure that windows are not easily accessible to young children.

7. **Use Cabinet Locks**: Install childproof locks on cabinets and drawers that contain dangerous items, such as knives, scissors, and chemicals.

8. **Anchor Rugs**: Use non-slip pads or double-sided tape to secure rugs and prevent tripping.

9. **Check for Choking Hazards**: Remove small objects that could be choking hazards from areas where children play. Keep toys with small parts out of reach of young children.

Educating Kids on Safety

1. **Teach Basic First Aid**: Educate your child on basic first aid skills, such as how to clean a cut, apply a bandage, and what to do in case of a burn. This knowledge can empower them to handle minor injuries safely.

2. **Emergency Numbers**: Teach your child how to dial emergency numbers, such as 911, and explain when it is appropriate to call for help. Ensure they know their home address and phone number.

3. **Stranger Safety**: Educate your child about stranger safety, including the importance of not talking to strangers, not accepting gifts or rides from strangers, and what to do if approached by someone they don't know.

4. **Fire Safety**: Teach your child about fire safety, including the importance of not playing with matches or lighters, how to stop, drop, and roll if their clothes catch fire, and how to safely evacuate the home in case of a fire.

5. **Road Safety**: Educate your child on road safety, including looking both ways before crossing the street, using crosswalks, and understanding traffic signals. Teach them the importance of wearing helmets when riding bikes or scooters.

6. **Water Safety**: Teach your child about water safety, including the importance of never swimming alone, not running near pools, and always wearing a life jacket when boating or near open water.

7. **Poison Prevention**: Educate your child about the dangers of ingesting unknown substances and the importance of not touching or tasting anything without permission from an adult.

10
RECIPES AND DIY REMEDIES

Creating homemade remedies and products allows you to control the ingredients and ensure they are safe and natural. This chapter provides recipes for herbal teas and syrups, homemade balms and salves, and natural cleaning products. These DIY remedies can help manage common ailments, care for the skin, and maintain a clean and safe home environment.

Herbal Teas and Syrups

Herbal teas and syrups are effective and natural ways to manage common ailments. Here are some easy recipes to get you started:

Chamomile Tea for Insomnia Chamomile tea is known for its calming properties and can help promote sleep.

- **Ingredients**:
    - 1 teaspoon dried chamomile flowers
    - 1 cup hot water
    - Honey (optional)
- **Instructions**:
    1. Place the dried chamomile flowers in a tea infuser or teapot.
    2. Pour the hot water over the chamomile flowers.

3. Let it steep for 5-10 minutes.

4. Strain the tea and let it cool to a safe temperature.

5. Add honey if desired.

6. Serve the tea about 30 minutes before bedtime.

Ginger Tea for Indigestion Ginger tea can help soothe the digestive system and relieve indigestion.

- **Ingredients**:

    ◦ 1 small piece of fresh ginger (about 1 inch), sliced

    ◦ 1 cup water

    ◦ Honey (optional)

- **Instructions**:

    1. Place the sliced ginger in a saucepan with the water.

    2. Bring to a boil, then reduce the heat and simmer for 10-15 minutes.

    3. Strain the tea and let it cool to a safe temperature.

    4. Add honey if desired.

    5. Serve the tea warm.

Elderberry Syrup for Immune Support Elderberry syrup is rich in antioxidants and can help boost the immune system.

- **Ingredients**:

    ◦ 1 cup dried elderberries

    ◦ 4 cups water

    ◦ 1 cup honey

    ◦ 1 cinnamon stick (optional)

    ◦ 1 teaspoon dried ginger (optional)

- ○ 1 teaspoon dried cloves (optional)

- **Instructions**:

  1. Combine the elderberries, water, cinnamon stick, ginger, and cloves in a saucepan.

  2. Bring to a boil, then reduce the heat and simmer for 45 minutes to 1 hour, until the liquid is reduced by half.

  3. Remove from heat and let it cool slightly.

  4. Strain the mixture through a fine mesh strainer or cheesecloth into a bowl, pressing the berries to extract all the juice.

  5. Stir in the honey until well combined.

  6. Pour the syrup into a glass jar or bottle and store in the refrigerator.

  7. Take 1 teaspoon daily for immune support.

Peppermint Tea for Colds and Congestion Peppermint tea can help relieve congestion and soothe cold symptoms.

- **Ingredients**:

  - ○ 1 teaspoon dried peppermint leaves

  - ○ 1 cup hot water

  - ○ Honey (optional)

- **Instructions**:

  1. Place the dried peppermint leaves in a tea infuser or teapot.

  2. Pour the hot water over the peppermint leaves.

  3. Let it steep for 5-10 minutes.

  4. Strain the tea and let it cool to a safe temperature.

  5. Add honey if desired.

6. Serve the tea warm.

Homemade Balms and Salves

Homemade balms and salves are effective for treating minor skin conditions and injuries. Here are some step-by-step guides for creating your own natural balms and salves:

Soothing Calendula Salve Calendula salve is excellent for soothing irritated skin, minor cuts, and scrapes.

- **Ingredients**:

    ◦ 1 cup dried calendula flowers

    ◦ 1 cup olive oil

    ◦ 1/4 cup beeswax

    ◦ 10 drops lavender essential oil (optional)

- **Instructions**:

    1. Infuse the olive oil with calendula flowers by placing the flowers and oil in a double boiler or a heatproof bowl set over a pot of simmering water. Heat gently for 1-2 hours, stirring occasionally.

    2. Strain the oil through a fine mesh strainer or cheesecloth into a clean bowl, pressing the flowers to extract all the oil.

    3. Return the infused oil to the double boiler and add the beeswax.

    4. Heat gently until the beeswax is completely melted, stirring occasionally.

    5. Remove from heat and add the lavender essential oil if using.

    6. Pour the mixture into small glass jars or tins and let it cool completely.

    7. Store the salve in a cool, dry place and use as needed.

Healing Arnica Balm Arnica balm can help reduce bruising, inflammation, and muscle soreness.

- **Ingredients**:

  - 1 cup dried arnica flowers

  - 1 cup olive oil

  - 1/4 cup beeswax

  - 10 drops peppermint essential oil (optional)

- **Instructions**:

  1. Infuse the olive oil with arnica flowers by placing the flowers and oil in a double boiler or a heatproof bowl set over a pot of simmering water. Heat gently for 1-2 hours, stirring occasionally.

  2. Strain the oil through a fine mesh strainer or cheesecloth into a clean bowl, pressing the flowers to extract all the oil.

  3. Return the infused oil to the double boiler and add the beeswax.

  4. Heat gently until the beeswax is completely melted, stirring occasionally.

  5. Remove from heat and add the peppermint essential oil if using.

  6. Pour the mixture into small glass jars or tins and let it cool completely.

  7. Store the balm in a cool, dry place and use as needed.

Moisturizing Lavender Lip Balm Lavender lip balm can help soothe and moisturize dry, chapped lips.

- **Ingredients**:

  - 2 tablespoons coconut oil

- ∘ 2 tablespoons shea butter

- ∘ 2 tablespoons beeswax

- ∘ 10 drops lavender essential oil

- **Instructions**:

  1. Place the coconut oil, shea butter, and beeswax in a double boiler or a heatproof bowl set over a pot of simmering water.

  2. Heat gently until the ingredients are completely melted, stirring occasionally.

  3. Remove from heat and add the lavender essential oil.

  4. Pour the mixture into lip balm tubes or small tins and let it cool completely.

  5. Store the lip balm in a cool, dry place and use as needed.

Natural Cleaning Products

Natural cleaning products are safe, effective, and environmentally friendly alternatives to commercial cleaners. Here are some recipes for making your own natural cleaning products:

All-Purpose Cleaner This all-purpose cleaner can be used on a variety of surfaces, including countertops, floors, and bathrooms.

- **Ingredients**:

  - ∘ 1 cup white vinegar

  - ∘ 1 cup water

  - ∘ 10 drops lemon essential oil

  - ∘ 10 drops tea tree essential oil

- **Instructions**:

  1. Combine the vinegar and water in a spray bottle.

2. Add the lemon and tea tree essential oils.

3. Shake well to mix.

4. Spray the cleaner on surfaces and wipe with a clean cloth.

Glass Cleaner This glass cleaner leaves windows and mirrors streak-free and sparkling.

- **Ingredients**:

  ◦ 1 cup water

  ◦ 1 cup white vinegar

  ◦ 1 tablespoon cornstarch

  ◦ 10 drops lavender essential oil (optional)

- **Instructions**:

  1. Combine the water, vinegar, and cornstarch in a spray bottle.

  2. Add the lavender essential oil if using.

  3. Shake well to mix.

  4. Spray the cleaner on glass surfaces and wipe with a clean, dry cloth.

Disinfecting Wipes These disinfecting wipes are great for quick clean-ups and sanitizing surfaces.

- **Ingredients**:

  ◦ 1 cup water

  ◦ 1 cup rubbing alcohol (70% or higher)

  ◦ 1 tablespoon dish soap

  ◦ 10 drops eucalyptus essential oil

  ◦ 10 drops lemon essential oil

- 1 roll of paper towels

- **Instructions**:

  1. Cut the roll of paper towels in half with a serrated knife to create two shorter rolls.

  2. Mix the water, rubbing alcohol, dish soap, and essential oils in a large bowl.

  3. Place one of the shorter paper towel rolls in a large, air-tight container.

  4. Pour the liquid mixture over the paper towels, making sure they are fully saturated.

  5. Remove the cardboard tube from the center of the paper towel roll.

  6. Pull the wipes from the center and use as needed.

  7. Store the container with the lid tightly closed to keep the wipes moist.

Furniture Polish This natural furniture polish can help clean and shine wooden surfaces.

- **Ingredients**:

  - 1/4 cup olive oil

  - 1/4 cup white vinegar

  - 10 drops lemon essential oil

- **Instructions**:

  1. Combine the olive oil, vinegar, and lemon essential oil in a spray bottle.

  2. Shake well to mix.

  3. Spray a small amount of the polish on a soft cloth.

  4. Wipe down wooden furniture to clean and shine.

By making your own herbal teas, syrups, balms, salves, and cleaning products, you can ensure that the ingredients are safe and natural for your family. These DIY remedies and products can help manage common ailments, care for the skin, and maintain a clean and healthy home environment.

CONCLUSION

Emphasizing the Balance

Combining natural and conventional medicine offers a balanced approach to healthcare that maximizes the benefits of both. Conventional medicine excels in emergency situations, surgical interventions, and managing severe conditions, while natural remedies can be highly effective for preventive care, managing minor ailments, and promoting overall well-being.

Combining Natural and Conventional Medicine Integrating natural remedies with conventional medicine requires a thoughtful and informed approach. Here are some key points to consider:

- **Consultation with Healthcare Professionals**: Always consult with a healthcare professional before trying new remedies, especially for serious or persistent conditions. They can provide guidance on the safety and efficacy of natural remedies and help avoid potential interactions with conventional treatments.

- **Preventive Care**: Natural remedies and lifestyle practices can play a significant role in preventive care. A balanced diet, regular exercise, adequate sleep, and good hygiene practices can help maintain overall health and reduce the risk of illness.

- **Complementary Use**: Natural remedies can complement conventional treatments. For example, using herbal teas to soothe symptoms of a cold or employing natural balms to aid skin healing while following prescribed medical treatments.

- **Holistic Approach**: A holistic approach considers the physical, emotional, and environmental factors that contribute to health. Combining natural and conventional medicine allows for a comprehensive view of health and wellness, addressing both immediate medical needs and long-term preventive care.

By embracing both natural and conventional approaches, parents can provide the best possible care for their children, leveraging the strengths of each to promote overall health and well-being.

Encouraging Parental Involvement

Parental involvement is crucial in ensuring the health and well-being of children. Educating and empowering parents with knowledge about natural remedies and preventive care practices can have a profound impact on their children's health.

Educating and Empowering Parents Knowledge is a powerful tool in healthcare. Here are some ways to educate and empower parents:

- **Access to Information**: Provide parents with reliable and accessible information about natural remedies and preventive care. Books, reputable websites, and consultations with healthcare professionals can offer valuable insights.

- **Workshops and Classes**: Attending workshops and classes on natural remedies, first aid, and nutrition can enhance parents' knowledge and skills. These educational opportunities can build confidence in using natural remedies safely and effectively.

- **Open Communication**: Encourage open communication between parents and healthcare providers. Parents should feel comfortable discussing their interest in natural remedies and seeking advice on integrating them with conventional treatments.

- **Role Modeling**: Parents can set a positive example by incorporating healthy habits into their daily routines. Children are more likely to adopt healthy practices when they see their parents valuing and practicing them.

Empowering parents with knowledge and skills not only benefits their children but also fosters a sense of confidence and control over their family's health and well-being.

Final Thoughts

The future of home remedies and holistic health is promising, with a growing recognition of the value of natural and integrative approaches to healthcare. By embracing the principles of holistic health and preventive care, families can promote lasting wellness and resilience.

The Future of Home Remedies and Holistic Health The interest in natural remedies and holistic health continues to grow, driven by a desire for safer, more sustainable, and effective healthcare options. Here are some trends and considerations for the future:

- **Research and Evidence-Based Practices**: Ongoing research into the efficacy and safety of natural remedies will continue to expand our understanding and validate traditional practices. Evidence-based practices can help integrate natural remedies more seamlessly into conventional healthcare.

- **Sustainable and Ethical Practices**: The growing emphasis on sustainability and ethical sourcing of natural ingredients will shape the future of home remedies. Consumers are increasingly aware of the environmental and social impact of their healthcare choices.

- **Integrative Medicine**: The field of integrative medicine, which combines conventional and complementary therapies, is likely to grow. Integrative medicine emphasizes patient-centered care and considers the whole person, including physical, emotional, and spiritual well-being.

- **Personalized Healthcare**: Advances in personalized healthcare, including genetic testing and individualized treatment plans, will enhance the ability to tailor natural remedies and preventive care practices to each person's unique needs.

As we look to the future, the integration of natural remedies and holistic health practices with conventional medicine offers a comprehensive approach to healthcare that respects and harnesses the best of both worlds.

In conclusion, the journey to natural healing and preventive care is one of empowerment, balance, and holistic well-being. By combining the strengths of natural remedies and conventional medicine, parents can provide comprehensive care for their children. Educating and empowering parents with knowledge and skills ensures that they can make informed decisions and confidently support their children's health.

The future of home remedies and holistic health is bright, with increasing recognition of the value of natural approaches to healthcare. By embracing these practices, families can foster a healthier, happier, and more resilient future. Through the integration of natural remedies, preventive care, and holistic health principles, we can create a balanced and sustainable approach to well-being that benefits individuals, families, and communities.

THANK YOU FOR READING

Your feedback is greatly appreciated!

It's through your feedback, support and reviews that I'm able to create the best books possible and serve more people.

I would be extremely grateful if you could take just 60 seconds to kindly leave an honest review of the book on Amazon. Please share your feedback and thoughts for others to see.

To do so, simply find the book on Amazon's website (or wherever you purchased the book from) and locate the section to leave a review. Select a star rating and write a couple of sentences.

That's it! Thank you so much for your support.